THE
WAR ON
TERRORISM

DAVID DOWNING

Heinemann
LIBRARY

www.heinemann.co.uk

Visit our website to find out more information about **Heinemann Library** books.

To order:

☎ Phone 44 (0) 1865 888066

▤ Send a fax to 44 (0) 1865 314091

▭ Visit the Heinemann Bookshop at www.heinemann.co.uk to browse our catalogue and order online.

First published in Great Britain by Heinemann Library, Halley Court, Jordan Hill, Oxford OX2 8EJ, part of Harcourt Education. Heinemann is a registered trademark of Harcourt Education Ltd.

Editorial: Geoff Barker, Nancy Dickmann, Louise Galpine, Christine Lawrie
Design: Ron Kamen, Christine Lawrie
Picture Research: Rachel Tisdale
Cartographer: Stefan Chabluk
Production: Séverine Ribierre

Originated by Dot Gradations
Printed and bound in China by South China Printing Company

ISBN 0 431 183635
07 06 05 04 03
10 9 8 7 6 5 4 3 2 1

British Library Cataloguing in Publication Data
Downing, David, 1946–
The War on Terrorism. – (Troubled world)
303.6′25
A full catalogue record for this book is available from the British Library.

Acknowledgements
The publishers would like to thank the following for permission to reproduce photographs: CORBIS pp. **5, 10, 12, 17, 22, 26, 27, 28, 59** (Sygma); Mary Evans Picture Library p. **7**; Popperfoto pp. **15, 20, 25, 33, 34, 35, 37, 38, 41, 43, 44, 45, 48, 49, 51 top and bottom, 52, 55 top and bottom, 57**; Topham pp. **9, 11, 18, 31, 47.**

Cover photograph of the aftermath of the terrorist bombing in Bali, October 2002. Reproduced with permission of Popperfoto.

Every effort has been made to contact copyright holders of any material reproduced in this book. Any omissions will be rectified in subsequent printings if notice is given to the publishers.

Contents

Words that appear in the text in bold, **like this**, are explained in the glossary.

Two declarations of war

In February 1998, representatives of several **Muslim** political groups held a meeting in Afghanistan. Their main aim was to overthrow the governments of those Muslim countries like Saudi Arabia – a religious state – and Egypt – a **secular** state but with a mainly Muslim population – which they believed had abandoned the true Muslim religion. But they knew that this was impossible as long as those governments were supported by the power of the West, and particularly the USA. So they had to take on the USA, and the weapon they chose was terrorism – the use of violence aimed at civilians – with the intent of spreading fear.

At the end of the meeting a statement was issued by Osama bin Laden, the leader of the dominant group, al-Qaeda. 'For more than seven years', the statement began, 'America has been occupying the lands of **Islam** in the holiest of places, the Arabian peninsula, plundering its riches, dictating to its rulers, humiliating its people, terrorizing its neighbours...' These 'crimes and sins committed by the Americans', the statement ended, 'are a clear declaration of war on Allah [God], his Messenger [the Prophet Muhammad] and Muslims'. In return, the groups declared war on the USA and its people. It was, they said, the 'individual duty' of all Muslims to take part in this holy war, or **jihad**, and to 'kill the Americans and their allies – civilian and military' wherever they could.

The US response

Of course, it is usually countries, and not groups, that declare war, but al-Qaeda soon showed that it was serious about its own declaration. Over the next three and half years the group launched a series of attacks against American targets around the world. The USA fought back, firing missiles at al-Qaeda training camps in Afghanistan and starting a global manhunt for Osama bin Laden. There was no grand talk of a 'War on Terrorism', because terrorists were not considered that important. Terrorism was a terrible thing, but it had been around for a long time. Everyone knew that al-Qaeda was capable of the occasional outrage, but no one believed it posed a major threat to the Western world.

Then came '9/11'. On 11 September 2001, members of al-Qaeda hijacked four American airliners. One was brought down, possibly by passenger action, but two others were deliberately flown into the twin towers of the World Trade Centre in New York City and the fourth into the Pentagon headquarters of the US Department of Defence outside Washington DC. Over 3000 people were killed.

Debris is removed from 'Ground Zero', the name given to the area of New York City destroyed by the terrorist attack on 11 September 2001.

On the following day, 12 September, President George W. Bush declared war on the terrorists. 'The deliberate and deadly attacks', he said, 'were more than acts of terror, they were acts of war.' 'Make no mistake,' he added, 'we will win.'

But how will those engaged in the War on Terrorism know that they have won? During the months following September 11 the aims of the war have widened considerably, causing many observers to wonder whether it can ever be won. This book examines the roots of the terrorists who were responsible for September 11, and considers how successful the war against them has been. But the first thing to do is to clarify what is meant by terrorism.

5

Terrorism

The word terrorism was first used in the late 18th century to describe the actions of a government. In 1793–94 the Jacobin Government of France scared its enemies into submission by condemning around 4000 of them to death by guillotining. This wholesale slaughter was called the 'Reign of Terror', and the entry for 'terrorism' in the *Oxford English Dictionary* of 1795 defined the word as 'government by **intimidation**, as directed and carried out by the party in power'.

But over the next century and a half the generally accepted meaning of the word gradually changed into something very different. The idea of achieving political ends by creating fear or terror remained, but the people creating the fear changed. The word 'terrorist' was less and less used to describe governments, and more and more used to describe individuals and groups who used violence against governments. By the mid-20th century most people thought of terrorists as wild individuals – people who used guns or bombs in their attempt to **assassinate** leading political figures – not governments who terrorized their domestic or foreign enemies. Over the last 50 years, however, it has become clear that individuals and governments are equally capable of terrorism.

Individual and group terrorism

Since World War II anti-government 'terrorists' have fallen into two basic categories. The first, relatively small category involved groups of people who wanted to overthrow the Western **free enterprise** system as a whole. They believed, despite evidence to the contrary, that individual acts of terrorism – mostly bombings and kidnappings – would bring this about. In the 1970s this category included the Baader-Meinhof gang in Germany and the Red Brigades in Italy, who targeted prominent businessmen, politicians and military leaders. These groups believed that terrorism was a legitimate form of political struggle, and were happy to call themselves terrorists.

The second category of anti-government 'terrorists' included groups and peoples, mostly, but not solely, in the developing world, who were fighting against what they saw as foreign occupation. They were as diverse as the IRA (Irish Republican Army) in Northern Ireland, Algerians fighting to expel the French from Algeria, **Palestinians** in the Israeli-occupied West Bank and Gaza Strip, and the ANC (African National Congress) in **apartheid** South Africa. In the course of their struggles many such groups resorted

Political assassinations

On 28 June 1914, Archduke Franz Ferdinand of Austria was shot dead by a young Serb named Gavrilo Princip in the Bosnian city of Sarajevo. This event, which triggered the outbreak of World War I, was widely considered an act of terrorism. However, assassinations of individual politicians or heads of state are not usually carried out with the intention of spreading fear, and are rarely acts of terrorism. When US President John F. Kennedy was assassinated, for example, the word terrorism was rarely mentioned.

A policy of assassinating all the members of a particular group, on the other hand, is intended to spread fear, and to deter others from joining that group. Women teachers in Afghanistan, for example, were deliberately targeted by **Islamic fundamentalist** groups in the 1990s. Campaigns of assassination like this are a form of terrorism.

An artist's impression of the assassination of the Austrian Archduke Franz Ferdinand and his wife in 1914.

to acts of terrorism. But they did not think of themselves as terrorists. They usually saw themselves as freedom fighters or members of an **armed resistance**.

Government terrorism

During this same period governments were also involved in terrorism. They were involved directly, ordering their police and military services to commit such acts, and indirectly, by providing the money, weaponry and training which allowed others to commit them. 'State terrorism' was the name usually given to direct involvement, 'state **sponsorship** of terrorism' the name given to indirect involvement.

Many post-war governments sponsored terrorists. During the **Cold War** between the USA and the Soviet Union, both **superpowers** gave money and arms to terrorist groups, and the

7

Soviets set up schools to train people in terrorist techniques. Groups funded by both sides were involved on opposite sides in the Angolan **civil war**, for example. Each superpower claimed that those it supported were freedom fighters, and that those on the other side, were terrorists.

Many governments have been guilty of state terrorism. They use their police and military services to create fear among ordinary people in a variety of ways. Rural communities are indiscriminately bombed, as has happened in the Russian province of Chechnya – a small Muslim nation which is legally part of Russia, but which has been fighting for its independence since the break-up of the Soviet Union in the early 1990s. People in towns are subjected to random attacks, arrest without trial and the routine use of torture, as has happened in Indian-controlled Kashmir. Mass rape has been used to terrify populations, most noticeably in Serbian-controlled areas of Bosnia. Governments always deny they are involved in terrorism, and usually claim their opponents are the terrorists.

Defining terrorism

Who is telling the truth? Is it possible to distinguish between terrorists and freedom fighters, or is it just a matter of whose side you are on? The *Penguin English Dictionary* (1965) defines terrorism as a 'policy of using violence and intimidation to obtain political demands or enforce political authority'. The US Department of Defence defines it as 'the calculated use of violence or the threat of violence to inculcate [teach by repetition] fear, intended to coerce or intimidate governments or societies as to the pursuit of goals that are generally political, religious or ideological'. These definitions have the same core: terrorism is using violence to create fear, in the hope that this fear will force a political change of mind.

Do these definitions go far enough? They make no distinction between groups and states, between times of war and times of peace, between civilian and military targets. Is any act of violence aimed at causing fear an act of terrorism? Most people through history have considered it justifiable to use violence against brutal, undemocratic governments or foreign invaders and occupiers. During World War II, for example, the French Resistance used violence to unsettle the German occupying forces in France, but they are now thought of as patriots, not terrorists.

Any useful definition of terrorism must set it apart from legitimate acts of armed resistance against tyrannical rule, whether domestic or foreign. This can only be done by distinguishing between civilian and military targets. In this way, terrorism is best defined as the use of violence to create fear among the civilian population; whereas armed resistance is the use of violence against military forces being used to impose brutal or foreign rule.

How do these definitions work in practice? Palestinian fighting groups have been trying to force Israeli troops and settlers out of the occupied West Bank since 1967, and over the years they have launched many different types of attack, including the shooting of Israeli soldiers on patrol in the West Bank and the **suicide bombing** of civilian targets in Israel itself. Most Israelis would call both attacks terrorist attacks. Most Palestinians would consider that both are acts of armed resistance to the Israeli occupation; but according to our definitions the first attack (shooting soldiers) – aimed at a military target, with the intention of opposing and eventually ending a foreign occupation – is an act of armed resistance. The second attack (suicide bombing) – aimed at civilians, with the intention of spreading fear – is an act of terrorism.

Israeli troops congratulate each other after completing their controversial search for Palestinian terrorist suspects in the Jenin refugee camp on the occupied West Bank in April 2002. Palestinian sources claim that many civilians were killed during the eleven-day operation, which also destroyed much of the camp.

Nelson Mandela, former president of South Africa, is seen by many as a symbol of peace, but in the 1960s the South African Government saw him as a terrorist.

It makes no difference whether those responsible are individuals, groups or governments. It makes no difference whether the act is committed in time of peace or time of war.
It makes no difference whether those responsible seem to have a good cause. Any act which targets civilians with the deliberate intention of spreading fear for political ends is an act of terrorism.

George W. Bush's definition of terrorism

There have been few more obvious examples of terrorism than al-Qaeda's attacks on American targets in September 2001. The victims were overwhelmingly civilian, and the aim – the only stated aim, in fact – was to spread death and terror. No responsibility was claimed, no demands made. All that followed was the threat of more. This was terrorism in its purest form.

The response of the US Government was to declare a 'War on Terrorism'. On 20 September 2001, President George W. Bush told the US Congress that 'our war begins with al-Qaeda, but it does not end there. It will not end until every terrorist group of global reach has been found, stopped and defeated.' As the weeks went by he extended the enemy to include all terrorist groups, whether or not they had a 'global reach'.

But how did George W. Bush define terrorism? It soon became apparent that his definition included acts that had historically been considered acts of armed resistance. On 28 October, he told journalists that 'so long as anybody is terrorizing established governments, there needs to be a war'. Terrorism, according to President Bush, was simply violence directed against those currently in power.

This was the terrorism on which George W. Bush declared war. His terrorists included real terrorists like al-Qaeda, but they also included groups fighting against **dictatorship** and inequality, and peoples fighting for freedom from foreign rule. The USA's allies in the 'war' included governments and peoples who believed that real terrorists like al-Qaeda were worth fighting, but they also included governments – like those of Russia, Israel, India and Indonesia – which were, it could be argued, currently using state terrorism to enforce unpopular occupations.

Two Japanese people walk through the ruins of their city, Hiroshima, after it was destroyed by an atom bomb in 1945 towards the end of World War II.

Terror from the air

The German bombing of London and other cities in 1940–41, and the Anglo-American **area bombing** of German cities that followed, were carried out with the aim of spreading terror among civilian populations, and making them less willing to support the war. The American atom-bombing of two Japanese cities, Hiroshima and Nagasaki, in August 1945, which killed well over 100,000 people, was carried out to terrify the Japanese into surrendering.

All these bombing campaigns involved states using violence against civilians with the aim of spreading terror for political purposes. As such, they were all acts of state terrorism. They were not, however, seen as such by the governments responsible, who claimed that such acts were permissible during a mutually-declared war.

Turning point: the rise of Islamic fundamentalism

The nineteen men who carried out the terrorist attacks on 11 September 2001 came from several different countries, but they had one crucial thing in common. They were all **Islamic fundamentalists, Muslims** who believed so strongly in their version of Islam that they were prepared to kill thousands of civilians and themselves on its behalf.

Fundamentalists are not just found in Islam. Christianity, Hinduism and Judaism have them, too. Fundamentalism sounds straightforward, but is in fact quite complicated. It involves a return to fundamentals or basics, to a strict interpretation of what the original holy books mean. Holy books like the Christian Bible or the Muslim Qur'an (or Koran) are full of rules which

Islamic fundamentalists have been protesting against Western power and influence in the Muslim world for many years. American flags are being burned and anti-US posters brandished at a fundamentalist rally in Amman, Jordan, in August 1991.

followers must keep, and fundamentalists insist that these rules are strictly enforced. Because, over the centuries, these rules have been twisted or adapted to suit changes in the way people live, the idea of returning to strict enforcement usually seems extreme. Both the Bible and the Qur'an, for example, forbid people to make money out of lending, but if such a rule were enforced now every bank on Earth would be forced to close.

What went wrong?

In any school, or any society, some people are more determined to enforce the rules than others. It is the same with religions. Islam is now almost 1400 years old, and right from its beginnings there has been disagreement and conflict between those who wanted to follow the rules strictly and those who wanted gradually to adapt them to a changing world. A modern economy, for example, needs women workers. Islamic fundamentalists interpret the Qur'an to mean that women should remain in the home as they had done in centuries past. Non-fundamentalist Muslims, on the other hand, interpret it as giving women more freedom so they can take part in the world of work.

Over the last few centuries the main source of change in the Muslim world – which includes North Africa, the Middle East, and much of Central, South and South-east Asia – has been the impact of the developed West. Almost all of the countries in these areas were ruled by one European power or another for long periods, and most were still dominated by Western powers after gaining their independence. The modern history of the Muslim world feels, to many Muslims, like an endless list of humiliations: the Western destruction of the Turkish Ottoman Empire in 1918, armed interventions by European powers during the inter-war years, Western exploitation of the region's oil reserves, the creation of Israel on what Muslims considered their own land, and finally the series of military defeats inflicted by Israel on the Muslim **Arab** armies.

Twentieth-century Muslims knew that 500 years earlier their great cities were as rich and sophisticated as any in the Christian European world, and many of them wondered what had gone wrong. Why had the Muslim world fallen so far behind the West? Two answers were suggested. Some Muslims believed that their societies had not adapted fast enough to a world of changing technologies, and had been held back by their traditions and their religion. Others argued that Muslim societies had adapted too much. By doing so, they had left the true path of God, and lost

Sharia law

Sharia law is the law of Islam. Its origins lie in the Qur'an, or holy book of Islam, and the Hadiths, which contains the sayings of Muhammad. Over the centuries religious scholars have turned the rules of behaviour laid out in these two books into a wider set of laws. Islamic fundamentalists tend to concentrate on the original rules and punishments. Some of these – cutting off the hands of thieves, for example – seem unnecessarily harsh to many of today's Muslims.

Sharia law is enforced in Saudi Arabia and Iran. Other countries – for example, Sudan, Nigeria and Pakistan – have introduced it in part. In most Muslim countries there are those who favour Sharia law because they believe it brings them closer to God, and those who oppose it because they believe it is out-of-date and inappropriate for the modern world.

His favour. These fundamentalist Muslims wanted a return to basics, to fundamentals. They wanted a completely Islamic society, one in which the law of Islam, **Sharia law**, was strictly enforced.

Egypt and Saudi Arabia

During the 20th century individuals and groups of such fundamentalists emerged in many different cities and regions of the Muslim world. In 1928, leading Egyptian Muslims, worried that Western influences were corrupting their youth, set up a fundamentalist club called the Muslim Brotherhood. This group combined political and religious discussion with sports, and by 1940 it had over 500 branches. During World War II it launched violent attacks against the British-supported Egyptian king and his government, and was banned. The regime was overthrown in 1952, but its successors also banned the Brotherhood. Presidents Nasser and Sadat, who led Egypt from 1954 to 1981, were Muslims who believed in more adaptation to Western ways, not less.

Despite being banned, the Muslim Brotherhood's membership rose, and in the late 1970s its members carried out a series of attacks on symbols of Western influence, like nightclubs and casinos in the Egyptian capital, Cairo. Many of the most extreme members set up their own terrorist groups, like al-Jihad. One member of this group was Aymar Zawahiri, who would later become an important member of al-Qaeda. Another was Sheikh Omar Abdul Rahman, who was jailed in the USA for planning the World Trade Centre bombing of 1993.

Saudi Arabia was set up in 1932 as a nation in partnership with the ruling Saud family and a group of Islamic fundamentalists, the Wahhabis. Sharia Law was enforced by the religious police, and Western influences resisted. However, the country's oil wealth brought foreigners into Saudi Arabia and paid for its

Thousands of Muslim worshippers attend afternoon prayers at the Grand Mosque in Mecca, Saudi Arabia, during the Hajj, an annual pilgrimage to the city. The Grand Mosque was the site of Islamic fundamentalist protest in November 1979.

citizens to be educated abroad. So-called Western habits, like drinking, gambling and sex outside marriage, became more widespread, among both the population and the 2000-strong royal family. Angry at these developments, a new group of Saudi fundamentalists seized Mecca's Grand Mosque in November 1979 and demanded the creation of a true **Islamic state**. They were defeated, but their example inspired devout young Muslims like the 22-year-old Osama bin Laden.

The fundamentalist revival

In Iran, fundamentalists overthrew the pro-Western government of the Shah in January 1979. The Islamic clergy took over from the politicians, and Islamic principles were applied to all areas of public life – education, law, the economy. Women's rights were severely restricted and opponents of the changes forced into exile, imprisoned or executed. The revolution's leader, Ayatollah

An inspiration

On 20 November 1979 around 400 Islamic fundamentalists seized control of the Grand Mosque in Mecca, Saudi Arabia. The group was led by a 40-year-old fundamentalist named Juhaiman ibn Saif al Utaiba, and its dramatic seizure of Islam's holiest place was intended as a direct challenge to the ruling family of Saudi Arabia. The Saud family were not true Muslims, Juhaiman claimed. He demanded the family's overthrow, and the cutting of all ties to the **infidel** (unbelieving) West.

Juhaiman and his followers were eventually driven from the Grand Mosque, after a battle which lasted two weeks and in which over 200 people were killed. Sixty-seven of the rebels were later beheaded in town squares throughout the country, as an example of what would happen to anyone who dared challenge the House of Saud. One 22-year-old Saudi, however, was greatly inspired by the rebellion. His name was Osama bin Laden, and he told a friend that 'these men were true Muslims and had followed a true path'.

Ayatollah Khomeini waves to supporters in Tehran, Iran, 1979.

Khomeini, called for Muslims in other countries to overthrow their own governments and set up similar Islamic states. He despised Muslim regimes that supported the West, and contemptuously called their religion 'American Islam' or 'Islam of gold'. Khomeini's victory in Iran encouraged and inspired other fundamentalists throughout the Muslim world.

Later in the same year another event gave added impetus to this fundamentalist revival. For several decades Afghanistan had been divided between those who wished to adapt Islam and modernize the country and those who clung to the old values. In 1978 the **communists** came to power and launched a modernization programme that outraged many traditional Muslims. **Civil war** began and in December 1979, the Soviet Union sent troops into Afghanistan to help its fellow communists. The Soviet Union's **Cold War** enemy, the USA, responded by sending help to the Afghans who opposed the Soviet troops. These fighters soon became known as the **mujahedin**. From all over the Muslim world, individuals and small groups of fundamentalists set out for Afghanistan to join the fight.

17

Turning point: the Afghan civil war

The Afghan **civil war** which began in 1978 lasted, with one short break, for eighteen devastating years. During that time a steady stream of **fundamentalists** from all over the **Muslim** world came to join the fight. They established contacts, shared their political dreams and learned how to use modern weapons. Afghanistan became an international school for guerrilla fighters and terrorists, and its people suffered greatly as a result.

Picking sides

The war began when the Afghan **communist** Government tried to modernize the country. Its programme included a **literacy drive,** better health care, land for the poor, advances in women's rights, and an end to the drug trade. Probably about half the Afghan people supported these policies, and half opposed them. The religious authorities – the **mullahs** – saw the government's programme, and particularly the increased rights for women, as a direct attack on **Islamic** values. They were supported by tribal chiefs afraid of losing their authority, landlords unwilling to give up their land to the poor, and drug traffickers keen to stay in business.

The Soviet military intervention was at least partly self-interested – the Soviet leadership in Moscow was worried that a fundamentalist victory in Afghanistan would spill across the border and create

Soviet tanks roll into Afghanistan during the invasion of 1979.

an upsurge among its own 40 million or so Muslim citizens, who formed large majorities in six of the fifteen state republics. The American intervention was less obvious, but just as important and just as self-interested. The USA wanted to damage its Soviet enemy in the **Cold War**.

Unlike the Soviets, the USA did not send troops. Along with pro-Western Saudi Arabia, it spent US$40 billion on training and arming those who were doing the fighting. These fighters were divided into many groups, some moderate, some fundamentalist. The Americans supported the fundamentalists, thinking that they were more likely to damage the Soviet Union.

A soldier for Islam

Osama bin Laden, the future leader of al-Qaeda, was one of the many Saudi citizens who travelled east to play his part in the Afghan civil war. In 1984 he and a Palestinian named Abdullah Azzam set up the Afghan Service Bureau, which recruited men from all over the Muslim world to fight in Afghanistan. This brought him into close contact with the Pakistani Intelligence Service (ISI), the Saudi Government and the Egyptian Muslim Brotherhood. They also set up training camps where American army officers trained Muslim volunteers in the use of American-supplied weapons.

Biography – the young Osama bin Laden

Osama bin Laden (1957–) the only son of Muhammad Awad bin Laden and his youngest wife, Hamida Alia Ghanoum. Osama's father was a construction worker in western Saudi Arabia until a chance encounter with the king at a newly-built palace enabled him to set up his own construction company, the Saudi Bin Laden Group (SBG). By the time he died in 1968, leaving 11 wives and 54 children, he was one of the richest men in Saudi Arabia.

Osama went to an elite high school in Jiddah, Saudi Arabia, but was not sent to college in the West like most of his brothers. He studied engineering and business at the King Abdul Aziz University in the Saudi capital, Riyadh, acquiring knowledge which he later used in building defensive strongholds in Afghanistan and in the organization of al-Qaeda. An enthusiastic Muslim, he took extra courses in religious studies at the university. He had just left college, and started work with the family firm, when the seizure of the Grand Mosque in 1979 inspired him to become a fighter for Islamic fundamentalism.

Bin Laden did his share of fighting. He was wounded during one military operation in 1987, and played a prominent role in the battle for Jaji in 1989. He was a rich man, having inherited at least US$25 million from his father, and his willingness to live an ordinary soldier's life impressed many of the Afghan **mujahedin** and their foreign Muslim supporters. As one mujahedin put it: 'he came down from his palace to live with the Afghan peasants and the **Arab** fighters. He cooked with them, ate with them, dug trenches with them'.

Osama bin Laden (left), founder and leader of al-Qaeda, with one of his right-hand men, the Egyptian Ayman al-Zawahiri, during an interview in Pakistan two months after the September 11 attacks.

Victory for the fundamentalists

By the mid-1980s it was obvious that the Afghan Government and its Soviet allies could not defeat the American-supported mujahedin. They could hold on to what they had – the major cities, and most of the roads during the daylight hours – but that was all. Meanwhile, the casualties were mounting and the war was becoming increasingly unpopular back in the Soviet Union.

It was also attracting a lot of hostile world opinion. The Soviet Government decided on a gradual withdrawal, which was finally completed in February 1989.

Much to the surprise of many observers, the Afghan communist Government survived for a further three years. This was partly due to its policy of appealing to moderate Muslims, and partly to the inability of the various Afghan fundamentalist groups to unite against it. Afghanistan contains several major **ethnic groups** – Pushtuns, Uzbeks, Hazara and others – and members of these groups usually belonged to different fundamentalist groups. These ethnic groups shared a religious point of view, but they had a long history of mutual distrust, and none of them wanted to see the others in power. When the communist Government finally fell in 1992 the infighting between the fundamentalist groups worsened.

By that time bin Laden had left Afghanistan. He was overjoyed by the fundamentalist victory over the Soviets, which he saw as proof that Islam was once more on the march and that the tide of Muslim failures had finally turned. He believed he now had the contacts and the confidence to build another sort of army, one that could take on Islam's other great enemy – the West.

The birth of al-Qaeda

During 1987–88 Osama bin Laden and Abdullah Azzam came up with the idea of an international Islamic fighting force, which would be composed of dedicated fighters who had been through the fires of the Afghan civil war. This new organization, which would eventually be known as al-Qaeda ('The Base'), would be a sort of Islamic rapid reaction force, ready to fight for the fundamentalist cause wherever it was most needed.

However, bin Laden and Azzam disagreed about terrorism. Azzam thought it was the duty of Muslim fighters to avoid killing women and children whenever that was possible, and stressed those verses of the Qur'an and Hadiths that supported his views. Bin Laden, on the other hand, was determined that al-Qaeda should become a terrorist organization. In November 1989, Azzam was killed by a car bomb in Pakistan, most probably planted by Egyptian terrorist allies of bin Laden.

Al-Qaeda

Osama bin Laden returned to Saudi Arabia from Afghanistan in 1990. He still had mixed feelings about the Saudi regime, which had given generous help to the **mujahedin** in Afghanistan. He may have hoped that the Saudi regime would now play a more pro-**Islamic** role in the Middle East.

If so, his hopes were soon dashed. When Iraq invaded Kuwait in the summer of 1990 it seemed possible that it would also attack Saudi Arabia. Bin Laden went to the Saudi Government and offered to organize a force of 5000 Afghan War veterans to defend the country. The government rejected his offer, and turned to the Americans instead. Bin Laden was appalled that non-**Muslims** would be used to defend Saudi Arabia, the home of some of Islam's most holy places. The Saudi regime and the USA now topped his list of enemies.

The stationing of American soldiers in Saudi Arabia – such as these, preparing for the liberation of Kuwait – enraged bin Laden.

Into exile

Afraid that the Saudi Government would take action against him, bin Laden moved first to Pakistan, and then to Sudan, where an Islamic **fundamentalist** Government was willing to receive and help him. He stayed there for five years, creating money-raising ventures, building training camps for Muslim fighters and terrorists, and putting together the global network that the world would later know as al-Qaeda. These activities were noticed by the Western intelligence agencies, and pressure was put on the Sudanese to expel bin Laden. In 1996 he moved to Afghanistan, where recent developments assured him of a welcome.

The second Afghan **civil war**, which had begun with the fall of the **communist** Government in 1992, was drawing to a close. Neighbouring Pakistan, eager for peace and the chance to send back several million Afghan refugees, had thrown its weight behind a fast-growing movement of Islamic fundamentalist students called the Taliban, which was led by Mullah Omar. By 1996, the Taliban controlled well over half of Afghanistan, and was happy to offer its fellow fundamentalists in al-Qaeda a new home.

Biography – Mullah Omar

Muhammad Omar Akhund (1959–), later known as Mullah Omar, was born in southern Afghanistan. He came from an extremely poor family, receiving his first pair of shoes when he was thirteen years old. He was educated at a religious school in the southern city of Kandahar, and began work as a village mullah (clergyman) in the mid-1980s. During the two Afghan civil wars (1979–89 and 1992–96) he fought for one fundamentalist group and then helped to organize another, the Taliban. During the fighting he was injured four times, and blinded in his right eye.

Mullah Omar was elected leader of the Taliban in 1994, and played a prominent role in the military campaign that brought the group to power in 1996. Extremely religious, he imposed the strictest possible version of **Sharia law** on the Afghan people. After the bombing of two US embassies in Africa in 1998, and again after September 11, he refused to hand his fundamentalist friend, Osama bin Laden, over to the USA. As a result, his government was overthrown by the American-supported Northern Alliance, a non-Taliban Afghan resistance movement, in November 2002. At the time of writing, his whereabouts are not known.

23

Reasons for anger

Why was al-Qaeda able to attract so many recruits and active helpers, and why did its actions receive support from so many Muslims? In the Muslim world many people believe that their countries are run by governments who look after their own interests first, Western interests second, and their people's interests a long way third. Many ordinary Muslims also believe that they are losing one world – the world of traditional ways and values – without gaining another – the world of Western-style prosperity that they see on television. They blame their governments for this, and they blame the West for supporting those governments.

There are also more specific grievances. Many Muslims believe that these offer further proof that they are being persecuted by the West. The most obvious is Western, and particularly American, support for Israel. They hear Western leaders demand that Muslim leaders obey **United Nations** resolutions, and wonder why Israel is not asked to obey them and allow the creation of an independent Palestinian state in the lands occupied since 1967. They see the Russians violently repressing the Muslim Chechens' desire for independence, the Indians refusing to allow Muslim Kashmiris the self-determination they were promised.

How al-Qaeda works

The al-Qaeda that emerged in the 1990s had a leader (the Emir General, Osama bin Laden), a ruling committee (the Shura Majlis), and four operational committees which dealt with military matters, finance, Islamic studies and publicity. This leadership structure

Oplan Bojinka

In 1994, an al-Qaeda group in the Philippines, led by Ramzi Ahmed Yousef, began organizing an incredibly ambitious series of linked terrorist attacks called Operation Oplan Bojinka. The main elements of the operation were the bringing down of eleven US airliners over the Pacific in a 48-hour period, and the **assassinations** of US President Bill Clinton and Pope John Paul II during visits to the Philippine capital, Manila. Evidence of the terrorist plan was discovered by the authorities in January 1995 when Yousef, mixing explosives in his Manila flat, accidentally started a fire. He and other members of the terrorist group were arrested, but their links to al-Qaeda were neither understood at the time nor thoroughly investigated.

A US Department of Defence photograph of an alleged terrorist training camp in Afghanistan, after its bombing by US planes in October 2001.

organized training camps and raised money for operations, but it did not command a large army of terrorists. Al-Qaeda was the international hub of the wheel – the rim was composed of many different terrorist groups, who operated in particular regions of the world. These groups came up with their own ideas and had their own members. Al-Qaeda sometimes devised and ran its own operations, but it was just as likely to fund an operation by one of the regional groups.

Al-Qaeda did have a core strength of around 2000 fighters, most of them veterans of the Afghan civil war. By the mid-1990s, many of these men had returned to fight in their own war-torn countries – Indian Kashmir, Algeria, Chechnya and the south Philippines. Others remained in Afghanistan, where they now formed a key component of the Taliban's army.

In the training camps which al-Qaeda set up in Sudan and Afghanistan, over 10,000 recruits (some estimates put the figure as high as 100,000) were trained in both military and terrorist techniques. The organization even wrote its own textbooks: the 7000-page *Encyclopaedia of the Afghan jihad* covered both military and terrorist tactics, while the *Declaration of Jihad against the Country's Tyrants* concentrated on terrorism.

The growing threat

The scale of the threat was slow to emerge. There was an attempt to blow up New York City's World Trade Centre in 1993, an attempted **assassination** of Egyptian President Hosni Mubarak in 1995, two bombings in Saudi Arabia in 1995–96 that killed 26 people, an attack on tourists at Luxor in Egypt in 1997 that killed 58. Al-Qaeda did not claim responsibility for any of these attacks, but was later linked to all of them.

On 7 August 1998, the alarm bells went off. Trucks loaded with explosives were detonated outside US embassies in the Kenyan capital Nairobi and the Tanzanian capital Dar-es-Salaam. Two hundred and sixteen people were killed in Nairobi, eleven in Dar-es-Salaam. The two bombings had been planned as suicide operations, but in each case one of the bombers was captured. Under interrogation, they admitted that al-Qaeda had organized the attacks.

On 20 August 1998, the USA launched **cruise missile** attacks on al-Qaeda training camps in Afghanistan and a factory in Sudan that the Americans claimed was manufacturing **chemical weapons**. Bin Laden escaped, having left one of the training camps a few hours ahead of the attack. In November of the same year, an American Federal Grand Jury charged him with 227 murders, and the US Government offered a US$5 million reward for his capture. The Taliban Government in Afghanistan was asked to surrender him, but refused to do so without proof of guilt.

Rescue workers with heavy lifting equipment gather outside the bombed US embassy in Nairobi, Kenya, 1998.

The wrong target

On 20 August 1998, President Clinton ordered a cruise missile attack on the al-Shifa pharmaceutical factory in Sudan, in the mistaken belief that the factory was producing chemical weapons. In fact, it was responsible for over 50 per cent of Sudan's medicine production. The destruction of the factory, and the chronic shortages of medicine which followed, resulted in thousands of deaths from malaria, tuberculosis and other treatable diseases. Many of the victims were children.

The Clinton administration eventually admitted its mistake, but refused to pay compensation. This issue was widely reported in the Muslim world, where it deepened resentment of what many felt was American arrogance. The mainstream US media ignored the issue, leaving most Americans unaware of the deep resentment their government had provoked.

Salvage workers sift through the ruins of the al-Shifa pharmaceutical factory.

On 12 October 2000, al-Qaeda attacked another US target. Two **suicide bombers** detonated a small boat full of explosives alongside the US destroyer USS *Cole* in the Yemeni port of Aden. Seventeen sailors were killed. One of President Clinton's last acts in office was to co-sponsor United Nations Resolution 1333, which named Afghanistan as the 'world centre of terrorism'. It also demanded the closure of al-Qaeda's training camps and the handing over of Osama bin Laden. In Afghanistan, the Taliban and al-Qaeda simply drew closer together. Planning for the terrorist attacks on the USA was already underway.

Turning point: September 11

On 11 September 2001, nineteen members of al-Qaeda simultaneously hijacked four airliners in the north-eastern USA. Their plan was to fly two of them into the twin towers of the World Trade Centre in New York City, one into the Pentagon headquarters of the US Department of Defence just outside Washington DC, and one into the White House, home of the American president. The fourth plane crashed into open countryside, probably after passengers tried to seize control from the hijackers, but the other three hit their targets, killing over 3000 people. It was the deadliest ever attack by a terrorist group.

The September 11 attacks were obviously a tragedy for the victims, their families, and their friends. It was also an enormous shock to peoples and governments around the world, many of whom lost citizens. The huge number of deaths was one reason, the sheer drama of the New York attack – seen by billions on television – another. The mere fact that such a catastrophic attack could succeed was stunning in itself.

The attack was also shocking for two other reasons. One was the chosen target: almost 60 years had passed since the last attack on the USA – the Japanese bombing of the Hawaiian naval base at Pearl Harbor. The last people to launch an assault against the American mainland had been the British in 1812–14 and the mainland had never been attacked from the air. The other was the source of the attack: the homeland of the world's richest country had been attacked by an organization based in one of the poorest.

The twin towers of the World Trade Centre in New York City, shortly after the terrorist attack on 11 September, 2001.

First responses

Shock turned to anger, and anger to determination. On 12 September, the **United Nations Security Council** unanimously adopted Resolution 1368, which condemned the 'horrifying' attacks and called on 'all States to work together urgently to bring to justice the perpetrators, organizers and sponsors of these terrorist attacks'. It also stressed that 'those responsible for aiding, supporting or harbouring the perpetrators, organizers and sponsors of these acts will be held accountable.' On the same day, President George W. Bush told the American people that the country was at war with terrorism. A few days later the United States Senate and House of Representatives passed a resolution (by 98 votes to 0, and 420 votes to 1 respectively) allowing the president to use 'all appropriate and necessary force' against any person, group or state involved in acts of terrorism, or in protecting those who were.

Al-Qaeda did not claim responsibility for the attacks. Bin Laden denied that he was responsible, but few believed him. On 15 September, President Bush named him as the prime suspect, and demanded that the Taliban Government in Afghanistan give him up. If they failed to do so, the president suggested, then the Americans would come in and get him.

Suicide bombers

Suicide bombers are people who are prepared to cause their own deaths in order to blow up other people. Sometimes they strap the explosives around their bodies, sometimes they simply carry them in a car or van. The September 11 terrorists used planes full of fuel as bombs.

Many suicide bombings over the last 30 years have been carried out by **Islamic fundamentalist** groups. They call such bombings 'martyrdom operations', because they believe that the Qur'an promises the dead hero or **martyr** an immediate entry into heaven. There are verses in the Qur'an which suggest this, but there are other verses which forbid suicide as un-Islamic.

Organizations which use suicide bombers are hard to combat. It is harder to stop an attacker who has no fear of death, and a dead suicide bomber cannot be questioned about the people who helped plan and organize the attack.

A different kind of enemy

'The American people need to know we are facing a different enemy than we have ever faced. This enemy hides in the shadows and has no regard for human life. This is an enemy who preys on innocent and unsuspecting people, then runs for cover. But it won't be able to run for cover forever...'
President George W. Bush, speaking to the American people on 12 September, 2001

Pakistan's problem

It was clear to the Americans that taking on the Taliban would be twice as difficult without the help of Afghanistan's neighbour, Pakistan. It would be much easier for the USA to attack Afghan targets if it could use Pakistani airfields and fly through Pakistani airspace. And in the event of an American attack on Afghanistan, only the Pakistanis could block the Afghan-Pakistan border and prevent the Taliban and al-Qaeda from escaping. So enormous pressure was put on Pakistan's President Musharraf to abandon his country's support for the Taliban and join the American-led War on Terrorism.

Musharraf was in a difficult position. A majority of Pakistanis – 62 per cent in one poll – supported the Taliban, and might rise up in rebellion if he sided with the Americans. On the other hand, the Pakistani economy was in dire straits, and the Americans were certain to cut off economic aid if he refused to help. Musharraf decided that he could not afford to upset the Americans. He offered full co-operation.

With us or against us

He was not alone. The United Kingdom stood 'shoulder to shoulder' with the Americans, according to Prime Minister Tony Blair. Most European leaders followed his example, with varying degrees of enthusiasm. America's traditional allies in the Middle East – Israel, Saudi Arabia, Egypt, Kuwait and the Gulf states (Qatar, Bahrain, Oman and the United Arab Emirates) – all pledged their support. Other important states needed American encouragement. China, Turkey and Afghanistan's northern neighbours, Uzbekistan and Tajikistan, were all given financial aid in one form or another. The Russians were promised that the USA would not criticize the brutal war they were waging against domestic rebels in Chechnya.

A New York resident holds up a photo of a missing relative in the days after September 11, hoping for news that he was still alive.

The Americans made it very hard for other countries to say no. On 21 September, Bush told Congress that 'every nation in every region now has a decision to make: either you are with us or you are with the terrorists.' Many governments supported neither, but were afraid to defy the USA too openly. They offered verbal support, and their votes at the United Nations, but not much else. On 28 September, the United Nations Security Council unanimously passed Resolution 1373, which set out in considerable detail what all states were supposed to do to fight terrorism. While some governments took immediate action, others dragged their feet. In the meantime, the Americans, with help from the British and a few others, made their preparations for a war in Afghanistan.

Bin Laden's threat

*'These events have divided the world into two camps, the camp of the faithful and the camp of the **infidels** [non-believers]... As to America, I say to it and its people a few words: I swear to Allah that those living in America will not live in security and safety until we live in peace and security in our lands and in Palestine, and the army of infidels has departed from the Land of Muhammad [Saudi Arabia], peace be upon him.'*

From a video statement issued by Osama bin Laden. This was shown on the al-Jazeera TV channel on 7 October 2001, the day US forces began their air attacks in Afghanistan. In this statement bin Laden seems to be implying that an American withdrawal from Saudi Arabia, and an acceptable solution to the Palestinian problem, are al-Qaeda's most important conditions for ending its war on the West

Operation 'Enduring Freedom'

On 7 October 2001, US and British forces fired 50 **cruise missiles** at Taliban military positions inside Afghanistan. This marked the start of Operation 'Enduring Freedom', the name given to the military campaign in Afghanistan. Its aims were to overthrow the Taliban Government, capture the leaders of al-Qaeda, and prevent the country from being used as a base for terrorists.

The American strategy

The politicians and military planners in Washington DC had a clear idea of how they intended to fight this war. They had two good reasons for keeping the use of US ground troops to an absolute minimum. In a ground war, the enemy would have the advantage of fighting in his own backyard. And the Government was worried that the American people would not accept high US casualties.

The map shows landlocked Afghanistan. The USA stationed warships at sea and used them as a base to launch attacks on Taliban positions during Operation 'Enduring Freedom'.

Instead of using large numbers of US ground troops, the planners decided on a combination of American air power, small **special forces** units, and ground troops supplied by Afghan opponents of the Taliban. These ground troops, united under the name of the Northern Alliance, had held on to small areas of the country during the Taliban's years in power. Now – with American air and financial support – it was hoped that that they would expand the areas under their control.

There were two potential problems with this strategy: the extensive use of air power was likely to cause a lot of civilian casualties, and the Northern Alliance was unlikely to be much of an improvement on the Taliban. Both concerns were proved to be justified: more civilians were killed during 'Enduring Freedom' than in the September 11 attacks, and despite the efforts of the new government to rescind many Taliban regulations, Northern Alliance behaviour towards the Taliban was often brutal, exacting revenge for the Taliban's own brutalities. But from the American point of view, the most important thing was that the strategy worked.

The war against the Taliban

During the first week of the operation the Americans destroyed the Taliban's air defences with missile attacks and night bombing raids. In the second week they were able to launch daylight bombing raids against the Taliban's army, including those units which were dug in north of the capital city, Kabul, in anticipation of a Northern Alliance ground attack.

Through the third and fourth weeks the bombing campaign continued, but the Taliban seemed to be holding firm. Then, on 9 November 2001, the Northern Alliance captured the key

Some regulations introduced by the Taliban

• Women and girls must wear a burqa (a garment that covers the whole body, including the head). They are forbidden to wear brightly-coloured clothes under the burqa.
• Girls and women are not allowed to work outside the home.
• Separate buses for men and women.
• Nail polish, lipstick and make-up are forbidden.
• Men must grow beards.
• A young woman must not talk with a young man.
• **Muslim** families may not listen to music even during a wedding.
• Displaying photos of animals or humans is forbidden.

Afghan women wearing burqas in the Afghan capital, Kabul.

northern town of Mazar-e-Sharif, and began marching south to Kabul. This was the turning point. American planes dropped huge quantities of explosives on the Taliban lines outside the capital, killing thousands in their trenches and putting the rest to flight. On 12 November Northern Alliance troops entered Kabul. It would take another month to dislodge the Taliban from their last stronghold in the southern city of Kandahar, but the outcome was no longer in doubt. One aim of the operation – the overthrow of the Taliban – had been achieved.

Successes and failures

What of the other aims? Leaders of the many Afghan groups met in Germany early in December to choose a new **provisional government** for their war-torn country. This government was full of people who had fought each other in the past, and the leader they chose, Hamid Karzai, would clearly have a difficult job holding it together. He was promised that Western soldiers would remain in Afghanistan to help keep the peace, and that his government would be given enormous financial help to rebuild the country.

Most ordinary Afghans welcomed the overthrow of the Taliban and an end to the restrictions that they had imposed. But it was not all good news. The drug trade, which the Taliban had restricted, was allowed to flourish once more by the new rulers of Afghanistan.

Al-Qaeda had been dealt a serious but far from fatal blow. Over 500 of its troops, and one of its leaders, Muhammad Atef, had been killed by American bombs. It was believed at first that bin Laden and other leaders were hiding out in the Tora Bora cave complex south-east of Kabul, but after bombing and searching these caves the Americans found no trace of them or their bodies. They did find proof, in the form of a video interview with bin Laden, that he knew about the September 11 attacks in advance, but this was small consolation for the failure to capture him.

New Afghan President Hamid Karzai (left), with German Chancellor Gerhard Schröder.

Biography – John Walker Lindh

John Walker Lindh (1981–) was born in Washington DC. His prosperous family moved to California when he was ten. He grew interested in **Islam** in his early teens, and became a Muslim at the age of sixteen. A year later, with his parents' encouragement, he left home to study at a religious school in Yemen. In 2000, he went to Pakistan, crossed the border into Afghanistan, and joined the army of the ruling Taliban. When Operation 'Enduring Freedom' was launched in the autumn of 2001, he was captured by the Northern Alliance before being handed over to US forces. Brought before a US court, the 'American Taliban' was charged with helping the enemy, and sentenced to 20 years in prison.

Many people in the USA were unsettled by the discovery of an American fighting with the Taliban. Until that point the War on Terrorism had seemed to be a case of 'us' and 'them'. But Lindh had joined the Taliban and fought with them against his fellow Americans. This put a very human face on the conflict. Many Americans were also disturbed by pictures Lindh's lawyers released. These pictures showed an obviously ill Lindh, naked and handcuffed, and raised questions about how Lindh and other prisoners of war were being treated.

John Walker Lindh, barefoot, with a Northern Alliance soldier.

Music returns to Kabul

'*Vendors did brisk business selling Iranian and Indian songs on cassettes as well as razor blades... Music shops clustered in Farashgar Street were open again and filled with young customers while the air vibrated with a cacophony of Afghan, Indian and Western tunes.*'
Journalist Dilip Hiro describing the Afghan capital, Kabul, after the overthrow of the Taliban in November 2001

The war at home

On 5 October 2001, two days before Operation 'Enduring Freedom' got underway in Afghanistan, a newspaper employee in the US state of Florida died of **anthrax** poisoning. Anthrax is a bacterial infection found in animals, that has been developed into a lethal weapon against humans by military scientists in several countries. The victim in Florida had received an envelope containing this deadly substance in the post.

Many Americans, understandably jittery after September 11, feared that this was the beginning of a new attack. When four more people died of anthrax poisoning later that month, and further samples were mailed to several American politicians, they were certain of it. The alarm spread to the UK, where one false alarm led to postal workers undergoing decontamination procedures.

The attacks ended without the culprit being caught, but the weeks of fear and uncertainty had come close to creating a national panic. Americans were scared, and they wanted their government to do something about it.

Non-military measures

What could the US Government do? How did a government wage a war on terrorism? It could send its armed forces after the terrorist leaders, but even if such an operation proved successful – and in Afghanistan it did not – others were bound to step into their places. President Bush's War on Terrorism had to be much more than a purely military affair.

The USA and other governments set out to discover how al-Qaeda and any possible terrorist allies operated, how they were organized, how they communicated with each other, and where they were based. They set out to weaken and isolate these organizations by denying them funds. All these were jobs for police and **intelligence services**, not the military.

There was also a defensive side to the War on Terrorism. Precautions were taken against new attacks. Prime targets like nuclear plants were given increased protection, and security at airports was tightened up. Vaccines and antidotes were produced in large quantities in case there was an attack using **chemical** or **biological weapons**. Fighter aircraft stood by ready to patrol the skies above many of the world's cities.

Postal workers in Liverpool, UK, are led to a decontamination unit after a false anthrax alarm in October 2001.

Many of these activities, and much of the War on Terrorism, took place outside the public eye. Governments knew that advertising them would help the terrorists, and might cause a public panic. In the USA it was decided that one person – a Director of Homeland Security – would be made responsible for coordinating all counter-terrorist activities.

New powers for the president

In order to fight the War on Terrorism, the US Government (and others, like the UK Government) argued that it needed more powers. Congress passed the Use of Military Force Authorization, which authorized the president to 'use all necessary and appropriate force against those nations, organizations or persons he determines planned, authorized, committed, or aided the terrorist attacks that occurred on September 11, 2001, or harboured such organizations or persons...'

A prisoner is taken for interrogation at the Guantanamo Bay naval base in Cuba, February 2002.

In October 2001, Congress passed the United and Strengthening America by Providing Appropriate Tools Required to Intercept and Obstruct Terrorism Act (the USA PATRIOT Act). This defined terrorism as acts that 'appear to be intended to influence the policy of government by **intimidation** or coercion [force]'. It also gave the government sweeping new powers to search through personal, financial and medical records, to keep people in prison without charging them, and to seize the property of people or organizations thought to be involved in 'terrorist activity'. A similar measure, the Anti-Terrorism, Crime and Security Act, was passed in the UK in November 2001.

In early January 2002, the first prisoners were brought back from Afghanistan. At least three were British **Muslims**. They were taken to a prison camp, called Camp X-ray, at the US Navy base on Cuba's Guantanamo Bay. The Bush administration denied that these men were either prisoners-of-war or criminals, because either status would have guaranteed them certain rights under US law.

Concerns about civil liberties

In the fear-filled atmosphere created by September 11 and the anthrax scare, most Americans welcomed these government measures. The American media was also broadly supportive.

Total Information Awareness

In November 2002 the US Department of Defence unveiled a new information gathering system called Total Information Awareness. This system, it was claimed, would search through data available on computers world-wide – credit card records, passport applications, arrest records, sales of items like guns, chemicals and airline tickets – for patterns that would help in the prediction of terrorist acts and the arrest of their would-be perpetrators.

Many people worried that the programme violated ordinary citizens' right to privacy. In May 2003 Pentagon officials announced that they were changing the name of the programme to 'Terrorist Information Awareness' in an attempt to alleviate these concerns. Few people believed that the name change was proof of an actual policy change.

As time went by, however, a growing number of American voices were raised in protest. The government, they claimed, was exceeding its proper authority, endangering both **civil liberties** and the American **constitution**.

These critics pointed out that the president could have used the Use of Military Force Authorization to attack Germany if he had wanted to, since several of the terrorists involved in the September 11 attacks had lived there. They argued that the definition of terrorism in the PATRIOT Act was wide enough to include George Washington and Martin Luther King Jnr., and that the act was being used to strip away legal and personal rights which Americans had always taken for granted. They added that the act did not even work – 1100 people had been detained, but none had been charged, let alone found guilty. They pointed out that the camp at Guantanamo, with its shackled prisoners and uncertain legality, was doing terrible things to America's image around the world.

In the UK there were new demands for the introduction of national identity cards, which everyone would have to carry. Supporters believed that these cards would make it harder for terrorists to operate; opponents claimed that they posed a threat to civil liberties. There were also calls for tougher action against 'asylum seekers' – people demanding safe haven from trouble in their own countries – because of fears that terrorists might use this method to enter the UK.

Turning point: 'axis of evil' speech

Until early 2002, the Bush administration received little criticism for its pursuit of the War on Terrorism outside the USA. Operation 'Enduring Freedom' had failed to catch those guilty of the September 11 attacks, but there was general international agreement that it had been necessary. By allowing its country to become a haven for terrorists, the Taliban regime in Afghanistan had turned itself into a legitimate target.

But what, or who, would be next? The War on Terrorism was clearly not over, but the Taliban had been the only obvious target. Al-Qaeda's leaders had disappeared from view, and it seemed extremely unlikely that another government would take the risk of giving them shelter. At the beginning of 2002, it seemed to most observers that the War on Terrorism would now become a war fought almost wholly by the police and **intelligence services**, not by armies and air forces. President Bush and his advisers, however, had other ideas.

Widening the war

On 29 January 2002, President Bush delivered his State of the Union message to the US Congress. In his speech he announced a widening of the War on Terrorism. Governments around the world were, of course, expected to stamp out terrorism within their own borders. But the USA now had a second goal – the removal of regimes which threatened America and its allies with **weapons of mass destruction**. He named North Korea, Iran and Iraq as states which were trying to get these weapons and described them as an 'axis of evil' that threatened 'the peace of the world'.

Over the next few months, North Korea and Iran were mostly forgotten as the Bush administration concentrated more and more on Iraq. There seemed little doubt that Saddam Hussein's government was trying to buy or produce weapons of mass destruction, but there was no obvious link between Saddam and al-Qaeda, or indeed with any **Islamic** terrorist group.

The Bush administration knew this very well: Vice-President Dick Cheney had admitted in September 2001 that no such links existed. Nor were they likely to. Saddam was the kind of **Muslim** leader that Islamic **fundamentalists** hated, the kind that considered power and ambition more important than religion.

Biography – George W. Bush

Forty-third president of the United States (2001–). Born in New Haven, Connecticut, George W. (Walker) Bush (1946–) attended Yale University, and like his father George Bush, made his fortune in the Texan oil industry. He served for five years as Republican governor of Texas (1995–2000) and won the controversial presidential election of 2000, defeating the Democrat candidate, Al Gore. During his first nine months in office he pursued a narrow America-first policy, refusing, for example, to join international attempts to halt environmental decline and create an international criminal court.

In the aftermath of the September 11 terrorist attacks he made significant efforts to create an international coalition for the War on Terrorism, and sanctioned the use of American force to overthrow the Taliban regime in Afghanistan. In early 2002, he turned his attention to what he called the 'axis of evil' (Iraq, Iran and North Korea). For most of the year he pursued an aggressive policy towards Iraq in particular.

Consistently high opinion poll ratings and a Republican mid-term election victory in November 2002 seemed to confirm that a large majority of Americans supported his policies.

President George W. Bush at a White House press conference in 2001.

An 'axis of evil'

'My hope is that all nations ... will eliminate the terrorist parasites who threaten their countries and our own. Our second goal is to prevent regimes that sponsor terror from threatening America or our friends and allies with weapons of mass destruction... North Korea is a regime arming with missiles and weapons of mass destruction, while starving its citizens. Iran aggressively pursues these weapons and exports terror... Iraq continues to flaunt its hostility towards America and to support terror... This is a regime that has something to hide from the civilized world. States like these, and their terrorist allies, constitute an axis of evil, arming to threaten the peace of the world.'
President George W. Bush, in his State of the Union address to the US Congress on 29 January 2002

Why Iraq?

Why did the Bush administration make a campaign against Iraq the focus of the War on Terrorism? There are several possible explanations. The simplest is that the administration felt that Saddam Hussein was building weapons of mass destruction. These weapons would be a threat either in the hands of Saddam, or if obtained by a terrorist organization such as al-Qaeda.

Another explanation may have been the Bush administration's desire to have a visible victory in the war. As the War on Terrorism dragged on it became harder and harder to focus attention on it and make people feel like the government was doing something to make them safe. Iraq was the most attackable member of the 'axis of evil'. The people of Iran, unlike the people of Iraq, were loyal to their government and likely to defend it against invasion. Any attack on North Korea, which was known to have weapons of mass destruction (unlike Iraq, which was only suspected of having them) would create a crisis in relations with South Korea and China.

However, many people speculated that the administration's motivations were less noble. Some critics said that attacking Iraq had nothing to do with terrorism, it was about justifying a huge rise in defense spending and gaining control of Iraq's oil. They believed that the war was staged to reward the defense and oil companies who had backed Bush's presidential campaign. These complaints were given more credence when Halliburton, a company Vice-President Cheney used to run, gained US$600 million from work related to the wars in Afghanistan and Iraq.

International criticism

Whatever the reason, or combination of reasons, for this new concentration on Iraq, it went down badly with many of the USA's allies. French Foreign Minister Hubert Vedrine, for example, accused the USA of 'a new simplistic approach that reduces all the problems in the world to the struggle against terrorism'. He asked other Europeans to speak out against an America which 'acts **unilaterally**, without consulting others, taking decisions based on its own views of the world and its own interests'.

French Foreign Minister Hubert Vedrine who voiced his government's concerns about the direction US foreign policy was taking following US president George W. Bush's 'axis of evil' speech in January 2002.

The new US policy was even more unpopular among America's Muslim allies. Few had any time for Saddam, but they failed to see how an attack on Iraq would help the War on Terrorism. Many believed that he was flouting **United Nations** resolutions and probably trying to get hold of weapons of mass destruction, but Israel was also flouting United Nations resolutions and already had nuclear weapons. Why was it the Muslim country which was being picked on? Some Muslim governments started distancing themselves from the USA and its War on Terrorism, which, they thought, was beginning to look like a War on Islam.

43

A new strategy

The Bush administration seemed unconcerned by the amount of criticism it was receiving from around the world. Through the first half of 2002 it seemed more than ready to pursue a 'unilateralist' approach. If others were willing to join its expanded War on Terrorism then that was fine. If they were not, then the USA would act alone.

There was no shortage of military might. The administration proposed, and Congress agreed, a huge rise in the defence budget. By mid-2002 it stood at around US$350 billion per year, roughly seven times the next highest figure, for Russia. There were about half a million US troops stationed at bases in dozens of foreign countries. The USA possessed 30,000 nuclear weapons, a navy larger than all other navies combined, and an air force capable of reaching and striking any target on the planet.

An American warship, the USS *Boxer*, leaving San Diego Naval Station, USA, for the Gulf in January 2003.

In the past, US military policy had been based on deterring or preventing enemies from attacking. Military force had only been used when deterrence or prevention failed. But times had changed. In a crucial speech at the West Point military academy in June 2002, President Bush said that the USA would no longer wait to be attacked. In some circumstances it would strike first. The War on Terrorism would now be fought against anyone who was thought to be threatening, or was even capable of threatening, the security of the USA.

Iraq – the story so far...

The West's problems with Iraq began in the late 1980s, when it became apparent that the government led by Saddam Hussein was trying to develop weapons of mass destruction. Until then, the Western powers had helped Saddam in his war against Iran and turned a blind eye to the brutal way he treated his people.

In 1991 Iraqi troops occupied Kuwait but were defeated by a wide coalition of military forces. The United Nations sent weapons inspectors to Iraq to ensure that Saddam was no longer developing weapons of mass destruction. In 1998 the UN withdrew its inspectors because Saddam was not allowing them to do their job. After September 11, anxiety about Iraq's weapons and the possibility that terrorists might gain access to them grew. In November 2002 the weapons inspectors returned to Iraq. The United States and Britain were not convinced that

inspection was working and argued that any delay in disarming Saddam would be dangerous. They believed that it was part of the War on Terrorism.

On 20 March 2003 a small coalition of forces invaded Iraq. Within two months Saddam's government was toppled, but his whereabouts remain unknown, perhaps unknowable, though many people believe he has been killed.

Saddam Hussein, the former Iraqi dictator

The global campaign

While the Bush administration and the world's media concentrated on preparations for war with Iraq, the original War on Terrorism – which many considered the real War on Terrorism – continued in the background. The drive to deprive al-Qaeda of funds was not going well. Some bank accounts had been found and closed and some flows of money intercepted, but there was no sign that bin Laden's organization was running out of money. Many European banks were reluctant to seize accounts without proof that the money was intended for terrorists, and there were still many in the **Muslim** world who were willing to help al-Qaeda. In August 2002, a **United Nations** report suggested that the war on the terrorists' finances was failing.

The search for bin Laden and the other leaders of the organization went on, but with equally limited success. Al-Qaeda's military commander Muhammad Atef had been killed in Afghanistan, but in the year that followed Operation 'Enduring Freedom' only

Predator

In early November 2002, an American Hellfire missile, which had been launched from an unmanned aircraft called a Predator drone, struck and destroyed a car in the Muslim state of Yemen. The six passengers, who included a senior al-Qaeda member named Qaed Senyan al-Harithi, were killed. Al-Harithi was thought to have been involved in the attack on the USS *Cole* in October 2000, and a more recent attack on a French tanker in the Red Sea. The missile and drone belonged to the US Central Intelligence Agency.

This attack raised all sorts of questions. It was clearly in line with the Bush administration's new 'strike first' policy, but it was just as obviously a flagrant breach of the usual rules of international behaviour. Six men were executed in one country by the forces of another. The two countries were not at war. There was no attempt to make an arrest, offer proof of guilt or arrange a trial. The USA acted as judge, jury and executioner.

It seems unlikely that the USA would accept such behaviour from anyone else. On the contrary, if a foreign government fired a missile at a car on an American highway, it seems fair to assume that the US Government and people would be outraged.

one other senior figure was captured or killed. This was Abu Zubaydah, the Saudi Arabian who managed the day-to-day running of al-Qaeda's entire global network. Zubaydah was arrested in March 2002 by a joint US-Pakistani team, after a gun battle in the Pakistani town of Faisalabad. He was expected to reveal a great deal about how al-Qaeda operated, but only his American interrogators know whether or not he has done so.

Two senior leaders – one dead, one captured – seemed a poor return for a global manhunt lasting more than a year. It was hard to tell how seriously these losses had affected al-Qaeda, and how the organization was doing. Bin Laden and others may have spent 2002 scrambling from hiding place to hiding place in the mountains of Afghanistan or Pakistan, only minutes ahead of their pursuers. Or they may have spent the year in a safe haven known only to them, busily planning new attacks.

More attacks

There was, however, no doubt that al-Qaeda in particular, and **Islamic fundamentalist** terrorism in general, was still alive. A terrorist attack on the Indian parliament in New Delhi in December 2001 killed twelve, and other deadly attacks took place in widely scattered locations between then and the summer of 2002. There were bomb attacks against two Christian churches, an American consulate and a bus containing French technicians – all in Pakistan. There were bombings in Indian Kashmir, Tunisia, Yemen and the Philippines. All of them were carried out by

A Christian church in Pakistan, after its bombing by Islamic extremists in March 2002.

Islamic fundamentalists, and most of them by fundamentalists with some connection to al-Qaeda. There was no indication that the War on Terrorism was reducing, let alone ending, the range and frequency of these murderous attacks.

Depriving the terrorists of support

By the end of its first year, the War on Terrorism seemed less than successful. Although many suspected terrorists had been caught, it was proving more difficult to successfully prevent terrorist acts. Stopping terrorism meant depriving terrorists of the three things they needed most – access to weapons, a place to hide and enough money to support their activities – and this was not possible without widespread support for the War on Terrorism. This support was not always forthcoming.

One possible reason for this was the continuing sense of anger in the Muslim world and a failure on the part of the US government to understand the causes of that anger. This lack of cultural understanding was clear from the beginning, when the military campaign against terrorism was initially named 'Operation Infinite Justice.' This phrase was highly offensive to Muslims since according to Islam, only Allah can provide 'Infinite Justice'.

Some people believed that the War on Terrorism was not a War on Terrorism, but a war on Islam. As evidence they cited

Russian troops on patrol in the Chechen capital, Grozny. It is claimed that the Western powers agreed to ignore Russian human rights abuses in Chechnya in return for Russian support in the War on Terrorism.

Biography – Pervez Musharraf

Pervez Musharraf (1943–) was born in New Delhi, India. After several years in Turkey, his family moved to newly-independent Pakistan. Musharraf joined the army in 1964, and served in the wars against India of 1965 and 1971, winning a medal for bravery in the first. He achieved the rank of general in 1998, and was widely believed to have planned the Pakistani incursion into Kashmir that triggered the Kargil War of 1999. Later that year he led the bloodless **military coup** that overthrew the elected government of Nawaz Sharif. He appointed himself the nation's 'chief executive', upgrading his title in 2001 to that of president. His support for the US-led War on Terrorism and Operation 'Enduring Freedom' lost him much support inside Pakistan, where most people sympathized with the USA's opponents. He allowed elections in October 2002, but imposed rules that made an Islamic fundamentalist victory impossible.

Pervez Musharraf.

situations in Chechnya, Kashmir, and Israel. In each of these conflicts there was no doubt that some Muslims were using terrorist methods, but so, the Muslim world argued, were the armies they were fighting. They saw these situations as Muslims fighting non-Muslim foreign powers who were occupying Muslim territories.

Gaining the support of ordinary Muslims was important for two reasons. Like all people, terrorists live in communities. If a government wants to catch a terrorist it must have the support of that community. Even if the community does not support the terrorist, it may not be willing to turn him or her over to a government it sees as hateful or unfair.

The support of Muslims around the world was also important to their governments. A Muslim government cannot support the United States if doing so marks it as anti-Muslim in its own country. This became especially clear in Afghanistan and Pakistan. As 2002 unfolded there was increasing resentment in both these countries at the continuing US presence. This led to signs that the Islamic fundamentalist groups were gaining in popularity. If

Al-Jazeera

The al-Jazeera (which means 'The Peninsula') satellite television channel began broadcasting from the Muslim state of Qatar in 1996. It was the first channel in the **Arab** world with an independent editorial voice, and it soon created a stir by openly airing criticism of Arab governments and inviting Israeli guests to discuss the Palestinian question. After September 11 it became the channel which al-Qaeda chose for broadcasting its messages, and two video tapes of Osama bin Laden were subsequently shown. This provoked American Secretary of State, Colin Powell, into suggesting that al-Jazeera be 'reined in', but the Government of Qatar refused to interfere. The station itself pointed out that it was just what the West had always asked for, an independent voice which was prepared to report all sides of any story.

these groups returned to power in Afghanistan, the terrorists could re-establish a base. If they took over in Pakistan, they would have access to Pakistan's nuclear weapons.

An alternative strategy

Many American experts on international politics were worried by the direction the Bush administration was taking. They did not believe that the War on Terrorism was an anti-Islamic crusade, but they realized that it looked like one. The mistake, these critics argued, was in widening the scope of the war, first to include all terrorists, and then the so-called 'axis of evil'. The aim of the war, they thought, should be the destruction of al-Qaeda, and all other policies should be brought into line with this.

They argued that other ways should be found of restraining Iraq, because a war would punish millions of innocent Iraqis for what their government was doing. They argued that the USA should pressure Russia, India and Israel into reaching fair settlements of their ongoing disputes with Muslim neighbours, and that Afghanistan and Pakistan should be given the enormous economic assistance they needed to make a new start. If the world's Muslims were given such reasons to believe that they were being treated fairly, these experts argued, then the supply of recruits and supporters to groups like al-Qaeda would eventually dry up.

An Indian soldier on patrol in Srinagar, Kashmir, where Muslim militants have fought a long war against Indian rule.

Daniel Pearl

In January 2002 American journalist Daniel Pearl was kidnapped by Islamic **militants** in the Pakistani city of Karachi. Pearl, the South Asia bureau chief of the *Wall Street Journal*, had been trying to investigate links between al-Qaeda and the so-called 'shoe-bomber', British terrorist Richard Reid, who had tried and failed to ignite explosives hidden in his shoe on a transatlantic airliner in December 2001.

The kidnappers sent the Pakistani authorities Polaroid pictures of the journalist being threatened with a gun, and then, a few weeks later, a videotape of his murder. Pearl's brutal killing offered a terrible demonstration of the dangers Western journalists now face in parts of the Muslim world.

Daniel Pearl.

Turning point: the Bali bombing

For several decades now, the beautiful Indonesian island of Bali has been a major tourist destination for Europeans, North Americans and particularly Australians. At around 11 p.m. on Saturday 12 October 2002, a van full of explosives was detonated just outside the packed Sari nightclub in the popular resort of Kuta Beach. Around 200 people were killed by the blast and the raging fires which followed. Several hundred were injured, many of them badly burnt. A large majority of the victims were Australian. Almost all of them were in their late teens or twenties.

Wrecked cars line the street outside the destroyed Sari Club in Kuta Beach, Bali, October 2002.

No group claimed responsibility for the attack, but it was generally assumed that **Islamic fundamentalists** had carried it out. The prime suspect was Jamaat Islamiya, an Indonesian group with links to al-Qaeda. A few weeks later, Imam Samudra, a senior figure in Jamaat Islamiya and the alleged planner of the attack, was captured by the Indonesian police.

What terrorism does

Richard: 'There were two blasts. The first one knocked everyone off their feet and everyone was scrambling for the exit when the second one hit and knocked everyone off their feet again. After the blast it was all black. Everything was charred. There was singed hair and skin.'

Paul: 'The bar I was in just blew up. All I could see was just red and orange, and there was this horrendous buzzing noise in my head. And I was just surrounded by wreckage. I think I'm lucky.'

Matt: 'There was complete panic, with people diving for the door and scrambling over each other. Outside it was awful. There were bodies everywhere.'

Hanabeth: 'I was dancing to Eminem, enjoying the flow, when I heard the first bang. Many people stood still, and then there was the second. It was an incredible force of wind and heat. Somehow I managed to climb out through the roof. I was in the street in a complete daze, yelling out my boyfriend's name, but I had a strong feeling that he was dead.

Eyewitness accounts of the Bali bombing from the Independent newspaper, 14 October 2002

Why Indonesia? Why the Sari Club?

Why had groups like Jamaat Islamiya, and Islamic fundamentalism in general, gathered strength in Indonesia? Ever since independence in 1949, this mostly **Muslim** country had endured a series of governments more interested in lining their own pockets than helping their poor and rapidly growing population. There was little or no **democracy**, and a large and powerful army was used to stifle any dissent. The Western countries, far from objecting to this state of affairs, befriended these Indonesian Governments. They liked them because they were anti-communist, and because they created ideal conditions – low wages, few rules and no **trade unions** – for Western businesses. Not surprisingly, many ordinary Indonesians resented this state of affairs. An increasing number turned to Islamic fundamentalism as a way of expressing their resentment towards their government and its Western backers. A few went even further and joined anti-Western terrorist groups.

Why did the terrorists choose the Sari Club in Kuta Beach? It was certainly an easy target, and full of Westerners. It was also a club with a particular admission policy – local people were not allowed in. The terrorists were not interested in saving Balinese lives, but they knew how such an admission policy would look to much of the world. A nightclub in Indonesia that did not admit Indonesians – what a potent symbol of Western arrogance and domination!

Worse was to come. All the victims of the tragedy were taken to local hospitals, but all the Western victims – who benefited from health insurance – were quickly moved on to modern, well-equipped hospitals in Australia and Singapore. The badly burnt Balinese victims – club employees and passers-by – could not afford this level of treatment. Their hospitals had no burns cream, no bandages, no painkillers. Once again, the rest of the world was shown the gaping chasm between the West and the rest.

Finally, there was the reaction of Western governments. They asked the Indonesian Government of Megawati Sukarnoputri to crack down on the terrorist groups. This involved giving more powers to the police and military. And since decades of corrupt and brutal behaviour by the police and military had contributed to the rise of Islamic fundamentalism in Indonesia, giving them more powers was likely to make matters worse, not better.

The lessons of the Bali bombing
The Bali bombing was a tragic but fitting end to the first year of the War on Terrorism. Firstly, the horrific scale of the attack, and the utter disregard for human life shown by the attackers, was a terrible reminder of why a war on terrorism was necessary.

But secondly, the attack showed how hard terrorism is to stop and it also brought an uneasy awareness of how difficult such a war would be to win. There are so many possible targets in so many countries, and they cannot all be defended 24 hours a day.

Thirdly, the Western governments' immediate call for a strengthening of the police and military showed why so much of the War on Terrorism has made matters worse rather than better. Giving more power to corrupt and brutal defenders of an unpopular system will create more terrorists, not less.

Fourthly, the Sari Club's foreigners-only admission policy, and the differing treatment of victims, showed why so many people in the poorer countries of the world deeply resent the West and its people.

From Moscow to Mombasa

Two events in late 2002 confirmed how difficult the War on Terrorism would be to win, with the nature of terrorist attacks becoming ever more unpredictable. In late October, a group of around 40 Chechen rebels seized control of a Moscow theatre and took the entire audience of several hundred people **hostage**. They demanded a Russian withdrawal from their homeland, Chechnya. If their demand was not met, the terrorists said, they would kill the hostages and themselves. On the third morning of the crisis, Russian security forces released disabling gas in the theatre and then stormed it. Most of the terrorists were killed, and over 100 hostages died from the effects of the gas. Despite the loss of so many innocent lives, the Russian authorities presented their operation as a significant contribution to the global War on Terrorism.

Children released by the Chechen terrorists during the Moscow theatre siege.

A month later, on 28 November, unidentified terrorists in the Kenyan city of Mombasa blew up the Paradise Hotel – a tourist hotel owned and mostly used by Israelis – and fired two missiles at an Israeli airliner taking off from the local airport. The missiles missed but sixteen people – three Israelis, ten Kenyans and three **suicide bombers** – were killed in the hotel bombing.

Relieved Israeli airline passengers were greeted with flowers when they arrived safely in Tel Aviv from Mombasa.

Prospects

Much of the first year of the War on Terrorism was spent simply trying to define the scope of the war. There was much controversy, for example, over whether or not the war in Iraq constituted part of the War on Terrorism.

The war in Iraq cost many civilian lives and failed to uncover evidence of **weapons of mass destruction** or links between Iraq and al-Qaeda. Many people believed that by expanding the scope of the war to include Iraq, Bush had alienated some potential allies and thus made terrorism more likely.

By November 2002 at least five al-Qaeda leaders had been captured. Osama bin Laden's whereabouts were unknown, but many believed it was possible he had been killed in the war in Afghanistan. However, events in 2003 made it clear that al-Qaeda had not been defeated. In May 2003 al-Qaeda took responsibility for two **suicide bombings** in Saudi Arabia. The bombings killed dozens of people, including at least seven US citizens.

Even if the war were only against al-Qaeda and other known groups, it would be a difficult war to win. But, as mentioned before, in October 2001 President Bush seemed to widen the scope of the war again. 'So long as anybody is terrorizing established governments, there needs to be a war,' President Bush told journalists. If terrorism is defined this way, as any violent opposition to a government, regardless of how corrupt or unfair the government is, then it is difficult to see how the War on Terrorism can be won.

Problem or obsession?

Many people believe the threat terrorism poses to the United States and people around the world has been greatly exaggerated. The attacks of September 11 were truly horrific. The loss of life was tremendous, and the sense of fear they invoked was horrible. However, in 2001 an American was five times more likely to be killed by a handgun than a terrorist, and fifteen times more likely to be killed in an automobile accident. Worldwide 24,000 people die of starvation every day. When these figures are compared to the approximately 2,800 people who died at the World Trade Centre, it is easy to see why the threat of terrorism is not a primary concern for many people around the world.

Police prepare to search a house in Manchester, UK, where a colleague had been stabbed to death during a counter-terrorist operation on the previous day. Only days before, traces of the deadly poison ricin had been found in a London flat in another counter-terrorist raid.

In the West, however, the shock of September 11, and the possibility that a group like al-Qaeda might gain access to weapons of mass destruction, has made terrorism an obsession for both people and governments. The governments of Western countries continue to insist that some **civil liberties** must be sacrificed to catch terrorists. It is unclear to what extent people in **democratic** countries will agree to these sacrifices.

In May 2003 Amnesty International, an international human rights group, issued a report saying that the War on Terrorism had made the world less safe, not more. 'The "War on Terror" far from making the world a safer place has made it more dangerous by curtailing human rights, undermining the rule of international law, and shielding governments from scrutiny,' said Irene Khan, Amnesty's secretary general. 'What would have been unacceptable on September 10, 2001, is now becoming almost the norm,' she said. Amnesty blamed the war not only for justifying human rights abuses, but also for distracting the world's attention from other serious trouble spots, including the Côte d'Ivoire, Colombia, Burundi, Chechnya, and Nepal.

The Muslim world

The great majority of **Muslims** believe that terrorism is profoundly anti-**Islamic**. However, it cannot be denied that a large part of the terrorist threat facing the world comes from Islamic **fundamentalist** terrorists. The existence of such terrorists is partly the result of recent Muslim history, which is full of deeply felt grievances. Such terrorists are made more dangerous by their willingness to die, a willingness that stems from their belief that such a death will ensure them instant admission to paradise. (However, like the Jewish and Christian Bible, the Qur'an actually states that suicide is wrong.) It is much easier to plant a bomb on a bus or an airplane if escape is neither desired nor intended.

There are some ways in which Western governments can work to reduce the number of Islamic terrorists and their supporters. First, they can start by attempting to find workable long-term solutions for conflict situations involving Muslims. This includes places like Chechnya, Kashmir, and Israel. Second, they can start encouraging democracy in the Muslim world, rather than supporting pro-Western regimes that oppress their own peoples. Third, they can put money and effort into rebuilding countries like Afghanistan, Iraq, and Somalia, where the War on Terrorism has taken a toll on everyday life.

Where do we stand?

It's hard to assess where the War on Terrorism stands at any given point in time. At the end of November 2002, after approximately one year of the war, there was a suicide bombing and an attempt to shoot down an Israeli airliner in Kenya. In his State of the Union Address two months later, President Bush announced that the US was winning the War on Terrorism.

Not over yet

'The war on terror continues…Our work is not done. The enemies of freedom are not idle, and neither are we. This country will not rest, we will not tire, we will not stop until the danger to civilization is removed.'

President George W. Bush launching his campaign for re-election, May 2003.

Muslim Kosovars queue for food from Western aid workers at a refugee camp in Kukes, Albania, 1999. Western governments, aid agencies and individuals do supply humanitarian aid to Muslims in crisis situations but it could be argued that Western attitudes often contribute to causing such crises.

In a line many people felt was inappropriate because of its 'tough-guy' tone he stated that 'more than 3,000 suspected terrorists have been arrested in many countries. Many others have met a different fate. Let's put it this way – they are no longer a problem to the United States and our friends and allies.' However, despite Bush's statement, suicide bombings continued in Israel, and the United States continued to get intelligence reports that terrorist attacks were being planned against it.

Al-Qaeda can be defeated, but terrorism in general may never be fully wiped out. Steps must be taken on a day-to-day basis to track down individual terrorists, to safeguard dangerous materials that terrorists use, and to keep a protective eye on as many conceivable targets as possible.

Neither the War on Terrorism nor the controversy surrounding it, are likely to end anytime soon. In November 2004 George W. Bush will come up for re-election in the United States. It seems clear that the presidential campaign of any candidate will involve discussing the War on Terrorism and how effective it may or may not be. However, it may be left to historians even farther in the future to make the final judgment.

Appendix
Chronology of events

1957 *30 Jul* Birth of Osama bin Laden

1978 *Apr* **Communist** takeover in Afghanistan ignites first Afghan **civil war**

1979 *16 Jan* **Fundamentalist** revolution in Iran

20 Nov Takeover of Grand Mosque in Mecca

27 Dec Soviet invasion of Afghanistan

1984 Bin Laden and Azzam set up Afghan Service Bureau to enlist fighters from around the **Muslim** world

1989 *Feb* Soviet withdrawal from Afghanistan

1990 *Aug* Iraq invades Kuwait; bin Laden's offer of help refused by Saudi Government

1992 *Apr* Communist Government in Afghanistan falls; second civil war begins

1993 *26 Feb* First attack on World Trade Centre in New York City

1995 *Jan* Oplan Bojinka scheme, involving eleven airliners, US President Clinton and the Pope is aborted.

25 Jun Attempted **assassination** of Egyptian President Mubarak in Ethiopia.

13 Nov Car bomb in Saudi Arabia kills five Americans and two Saudis.

1996 *25 Jun* Car bomb in Saudi Arabia kills nineteen members of US Air Force.

27 Sep Taliban takes Afghan capital Kabul.

1997 *17 Nov* Fifty-eight tourists killed by terrorist attack at Luxor in Egypt

1998 *23 Feb* Al-Qaeda declares war on the USA.

7 Aug Bombing of US embassies in Nairobi and Dar-es-Salaam.

20 Aug US attack on al-Qaeda bases in Afghanistan and al-Shifa plant in Sudan.

4 Nov US Grand Jury indicts (formally charges) bin Laden for 227 murders.

2000 *12 Oct* Terrorist attack on USS *Cole* in Aden Harbour, Yemen.

Dec UN Resolution 1333 describes Taliban regime as 'world centre of terrorism'.

2001 *11 Sep* Attacks on New York City and the Pentagon.

12 Sep UN Resolution 1368 condemns attacks. US Congress gives president 'all powers'.

15 Sep Bin Laden named as prime suspect in September 11 attacks.

21 Sep George W. Bush delivers 'with us or against us' speech.

28 Sep UN Resolution 1373 sets out global anti-terrorism agenda.

5 Oct First **anthrax** death in the USA – panic lasts into late November.

7 Oct Operation 'Enduring Freedom' begins in Afghanistan. Al-Jazeera TV station shows bin Laden video statement.

15 Oct New UK anti-terrorist legislation.

26 Oct USA PATRIOT Act.

12 Nov Kabul abandoned by Taliban.

13 Dec Terrorist attack on Indian Parliament.

2002 *11 Jan* First detainees arrive at Guantanamo Bay, Cuba.

29 Jan George W. Bush delivers 'axis of evil' speech.

28 Mar Abu Zubaydah captured in Pakistan.

11 Apr Lorry bomb kills seventeen on Tunisian island of Djerba, including eleven Germans.

21 Apr Bombing in Philippines.

8 May Fourteen French technicians killed by **suicide bomber** in Karachi.

1 June George W. Bush announces new strategic doctrine in West Point speech.

13 June Hamid Karzai becomes president of Afghanistan.

14 Oct Bali bombing kills almost 200 people.

18 Oct Bombings in Philippines.

23 Oct Moscow theatre hostage-taking.

5 Nov Predator drone attack in Yemen.

28 Nov Suicide bombing and attempt to shoot down airliner in Mombasa, Kenya.

2003 *20 March* Coalition forces invade Iraq.

12 May Suicide bombings in Saudi Arabia kill 35 people.

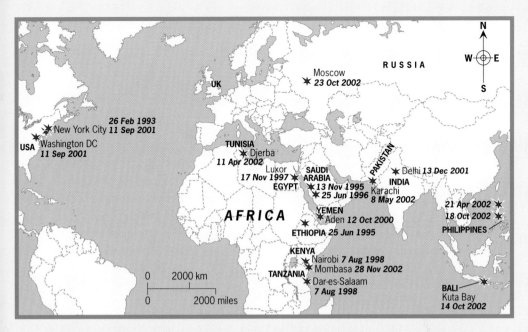

This map shows the location of many of the terrorist attacks in the 'Chronology of events' section.

Further reading

Ansary, Tamim, *West of Kabul, East of New York* (Picador, 2003)
Louis, Nancy, *Osama bin Laden* (Abdo Publishing Company, 2002)
Sinclair, Andrew, *An Anatomy of Terror* (Macmillan, 2003)
Woolf, Alex, *21st Century Debates: Terrorism* (Hodder Children's Books, 2003)

A useful guide to this and other recent international conflicts is Patrick Brogan's *World Conflicts* (Bloomsbury, 1998)

Useful websites

http://news.bbc.co.uk
  BBC news
http://www.ccr-ny.org/
  Centre for Constitutional Rights (USA)
http://www.cnn.com/WORLD
  CNN news
http://www.guardian.co.uk/usa/story/0,12271,797999,00.html
  Al Gore's 23/9/02 speech, which offers a reasoned critique of the Bush administration's conduct of the War on Terrorism.

Glossary

anthrax bacterial disease in sheep or cattle which has been developed into a biological weapon for use against humans

apartheid the keeping separate of races of different colours in one country

Arab people who live in an area stretching from North Africa to the Middle East. Arabs are often, but not always, Muslims.

area bombing heavy bombing over a large area, not aimed at a specific target within it

armed resistance fighting against a government which is unwanted, because it represents a foreign power or only a narrow section of the society

assassinate murder for political reasons

biological weapons weapons employing viruses or bacteria found in nature

chemical weapons weapons employing synthetic poisons

civil liberties those freedoms of action and speech which are considered necessary for the proper functioning of a democratic society

civil war war between different groups within one country

Cold War name given to the hostility that existed between the free enterprise capitalist and the communist worlds between 1947 and the late 1980s

communists believers in communism, a political theory and practice which puts the interests of society as a whole above the interests of individuals

constitution in politics, the way a country is set up to safeguard its fundamental principles

cruise missile missile which can be fired from land, sea or air, and which can be guided while in flight

democracy political system in which governments are regularly elected by the mass of the people, or a country in which this system exists

dictatorship government by an individual (called a dictator) or a small group that does not allow the mass of the people any say in how their country is run

ethnic group relating to different tribal or racial groups

free enterprise continuing of trade or business without much government control or interference

fundamentalism returning to the basics of a religion, which often involves taking more extreme social and political positions

hostage person seized with the intention of forcing others to act in a certain way

infidel (what Muslims call) a non-believer

intelligence services secret agencies which seek out information and try to counter enemies, both in their own countries and abroad

intimidation causing fear, often through violence or threats of violence

Islam one of the world's three major monotheistic (one God) religions (along with Christianity and Judaism), founded by the Prophet Muhammad in the 7th century

Islamic state state which bases its laws on those of Islam

jihad war on behalf of Islam

literacy drive an attempt to increase the number of people who can read and write

martyr someone who suffers or dies for a religious faith

militant someone who is prepared to take part in a war or armed struggle

military coup seizure of power by the country's armed forces

mujahedin soldier fighting for Islam fundamentalism

mullah Islamic clergyman

Muslim follower of Islam

Palestinians Arabs expelled from Palestine by the Israelis during the 1948 war

provisional government temporary government set up prior to creating a permanent government

ricin deadly poison that can refined into a powder or liquid that can be delivered as an aerosol spray, ingested or injected

secular concerned with social or worldly attitudes rather than religious ones

Security Council council within the United Nations most responsible for the maintenance of world peace and security. It has five permanent members – the USA, Russia, the UK, France and China – and ten rotating members chosen from other member states.

Sharia law Islamic law

special forces small groups of soldiers with special skills

sponsorship supporting with money and other forms of help

suicide bombing a bombing in which the bomber deliberately kills him or herself in the attempt to kill others

superpower a country with immense economic and political influence and military (including nuclear) strength; usually refers to the USA and the (former) Soviet Union

trade union organization to protect and improve workers' rights, pay and conditions

unilateral one-sided

United Nations international body set up in 1945 to promote peace and co-operation between states

weapons of mass destruction weapons capable of killing thousands, or laying waste large areas, at a single blow. They are usually subdivided into nuclear, chemical and biological weapons.

Index

Titles in the *Troubled World* series include:

Hardback   0 431 18364 3

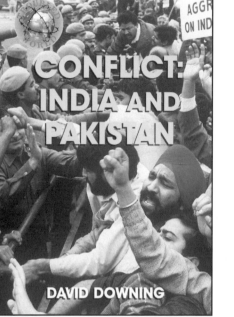

Hardback   0 431 18362 7

Hardback   0 431 18365 1

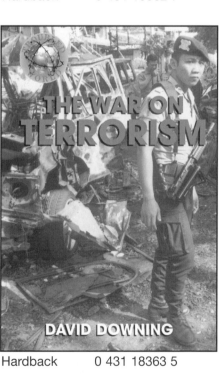

Hardback   0 431 18363 5

Find out about the other titles in this series on our website www.heinemann.co.uk/library